I WANT THAT ROOM!

HODDER
Wayland

an imprint of Hodder Children's Books

New Experiences

Are We There Yet? My First Holiday
Can I Feed It? My First Pet
I Want That Room! Moving House
I'm Still Important! A New Baby
Open Wide! My First Trip to the Dentist
Say Aah! My First Visit to the Doctor
Where's My Peg? My First Day at School
Where's My Present? My First Party

Published in Great Britain in 2000 by Hodder Wayland, an imprint of Hodder Children's Books
© Copyright 2000 Hodder Wayland

Editor: Jason Hook
Designer: Tessa Barwick

A Catalogue record for this book is available from the British Library.

ISBN 0 7502 2505 X

Printed and bound in Italy by G. Canale & C.Sp.A., Turin

Hodder Children's Books
A division of Hodder Headline Limited
338 Euston Road, London NW1 3BH

I WANT THAT ROOM!

Moving House

Written by Jen Green

Illustrated by Mike Gordon

HODDER
Wayland

an imprint of Hodder Children's Books

Mum and Dad had a surprise for me and my sister Emily. 'We're moving house!' Mum said.

'You two are so big now,' said Dad.
'We need more space.'

I felt excited, but a bit worried.
'What is our new house like?'
I asked. 'Is Goldie coming?'

'It's bigger than this one.' said Dad.
'There's lots of room for Goldie.'

Emily and I were sad about leaving our old room. We didn't want to leave our toys.

'Is it far away?' I asked. 'Will we still see our friends?'

'You and Emily will each have your own room,' Mum said. 'You can take all your things.'

'And you can still see your friends.'

11

Next day we went to see the new house. We met Mr and Mrs Jones, who were selling it to Mum and Dad.

Our new home had
a beautiful garden.

'I want that room!' I said. But Dad said that was Emily's bedroom.

'This is your room,' said
Dad. It was brilliant!

We went shopping to buy things for our new home. Mum and Emily bought tools for the garden.

Dad and I chose paint and curtains for my room.

The next week was very busy. We met the family who were buying our house.

Mum and Dad packed all our things in boxes. Emily and I packed our toys.

Our old home looked
strange and empty.
'Goodbye, old house,' said Mum.

I said goodbye to my friend Peter, who lived in our street.

See you next week!

21

Next day, we got up early. Two men arrived in a big van, and we loaded everything in.

Dad and I rode in the van.
Mum and Emily took Goldie.

At our
new house, we
unloaded the van.
Jim the driver lent
me his cap.

24

Everything was very messy. Later we all had pizza.

25

Next day,
Emily helped
Mum in the garden.

Dad and I painted my room. Slowly our new house began to look like a home.

Then the doorbell rang. It was the family who lived next door. I showed them my new room.

Notes for parents and teachers

This book introduces children to the experience of moving house. Parents or teachers who read the book with children, either individually or in groups, may find it useful to stop and discuss issues as they come up in the text.

Moving house brings change and upheaval which affect all family members, including young children. When houses are bought and sold, things often remain uncertain right up to the time of the move. New challenges may include practical matters such as sorting out possessions and packing, emotional issues such as saying goodbye to neighbours and making new friends, and major changes such as moving schools.

In the period leading up to and after the move, your child may feel excited, anxious, insecure, upset, sad, bored, or a mixture of all these. He or she may react to stress and change by becoming difficult, angry, demanding, withdrawn, or wakeful at night. Talking about feelings nearly always helps. Think about the reasons behind your child's behaviour, be patient and accommodating wherever possible, and try not to overreact.

Children who have recently moved house might like to talk about their own experiences and feelings. How do they differ from those described in the book? Encourage children to tell the story of their move, using the book as a framework. The stories could be put together to make a class or group book.

The experience of moving house may introduce children to a number of unfamiliar words, including estate agent, contract, survey, mortgage, loan, building society. Make a list of all the new words and explain what they mean.

Reread the story, encouraging the children to take the role of different characters. Talk about all the different professionals who are involved in the process of moving house, including solicitors, surveyors, estate agents and bank managers. Explain what all these people do. Discuss the signs and notices that estate agents use, and how these help in selling houses.

Use this book for teaching literacy

This book can help you in the literacy hour in the following ways:

✓ Children can write simple stories linked to personal experience using the language of the text in this book as a model for their own writing. (Year 1, Term 3: Non-fiction writing composition.)

✓ Children can look through the book and try to locate verbs with past and present tense endings. (Year 1, Term 3: Word recognition, graphic knowledge and spelling.)

✓ Use of speech bubbles shows a different way of presenting text. (Year 2, Term 2: Sentence construction and punctuation.)

Books to read

Moving House by Anne Civardi and Stephen Cartright (Usborne Publishing, 1985). Sam and Sophie Spark and their family are moving house. The books describes the busy days that lead up to the move.

Bad Boris Moves House by Susie Jenkin-Pearce (Hutchinson, 1991). Boris the elephant has outgrown his home. His friend Maisie decides they must move, but Boris doesn't want to! At the new house, everything is in the wrong place, and Maisie gets upset. Boris must help to sort things out.

Berenstain Bears' Moving Day by Stan and Jan Berenstain. The Berenstain bears are moving from their cave to a tree-house in the valley. The book tells how the move goes, how the bears make new friends, and how they stay in touch with old neighbours.

Meg and Jack Are Moving by Paul Dowling (Collins Picture Lions, 1991). Meg and Jack move house. The book describes how they pack up, say goodbye and settle into their new home.